Unscrollable

Unscrollable

Richard Fields

CONTENTS

1

Introduction: The Age of Algorithm Fatigue

For small business owners, the promise of social media was once irresistible. Platforms like Instagram, Facebook, and TikTok offered a level playing field—a place where creativity and authenticity could thrive without the need for a massive marketing budget. But over time, something shifted. The algorithms that once connected businesses with their audiences now seem to work against them. Organic reach has plummeted, engagement rates have dwindled, and the pressure to "play the algorithm game" has left many feeling exhausted and disillusioned. This phenomenon has a name: algorithm fatigue.

In this chapter, we'll explore what algorithm fatigue is, why it's happening, and how small businesses can break free from the endless cycle of chasing digital engagement. More importantly, we'll introduce the offline-first movement—a growing trend that prioritizes real-world connections over algorithmic whims—and explain why it's not just an alternative, but a necessity for sustainable growth.

What is Algorithm Fatigue?

Algorithm fatigue is the frustration and burnout that comes from trying to keep up with the ever-changing rules of social media platforms. It's the sinking feeling when a post that once would have reached hundreds of your followers now barely scratches double digits. It's the exhaustion of constantly tweaking content, testing new formats, and still seeing diminishing returns.

The numbers tell a sobering story. In 2012, a Facebook post from a business page could reach an average of 16% of its followers. Today, that number hovers around 5%. On Instagram, organic reach has declined by nearly 50% since 2020. For small businesses, these shifts aren't just inconvenient—they're existential. Without paid promotion, visibility is increasingly out of reach.

Take Sarah, the owner of a boutique bakery in Austin. She used to rely on Instagram to showcase her latest creations, and for years, it worked. But as the platform's algorithm began prioritizing Reels and paid content, her beautifully styled photos of croissants and cakes stopped getting traction. "I felt like I was shouting into a void," she says. "I was spending hours creating content, but my actual customers—the people who came into my shop—hadn't seen any of it."

Sarah's story isn't unique. Across industries, small business owners are grappling with the same challenge: how to stay visible in a system that seems designed to keep them invisible unless they pay to play.

The Origins of Algorithm Fatigue

To understand how we got here, we need to look back at the evolution of social media algorithms. In the early days, platforms like Facebook and Twitter used simple chronological feeds. If you posted something, your followers saw it—no tricks, no hidden formulas. But as these platforms grew, so did the volume of content. To manage the flood, algorithms were introduced to prioritize posts based on engagement, relevance, and, eventually, profitability.

The shift was gradual but profound. By the mid-2010s, platforms began favoring content that kept users scrolling—videos, viral trends, and, crucially, paid ads. For businesses, this meant that organic reach was no longer a given. The algorithms became gatekeepers, determining who saw what and when.

This created a double-edged sword. On one hand, algorithms helped businesses reach highly targeted audiences. On the other, they turned social media into a pay-to-play arena where only those with deep pockets or viral luck could thrive. Small businesses, with their limited budgets, were left scrambling to keep up.

The result? A growing sense of disillusionment. "I used to love social media," says Miguel, who runs a handmade leather goods shop in Portland. "Now it feels like a slot machine—you pour time and money into it, and most of the time, you walk away with nothing."

The Offline-First Movement

Amid this frustration, a counter-movement is gaining momentum: offline-first marketing. This approach flips the script by prioritizing real-world interactions over digital ones. It's about building relationships through in-person events, print media, direct mail, and community partnerships—strategies that don't rely on algorithms to succeed.

Consider the success of The Booksmith, an independent bookstore in San Francisco. Instead of relying solely on social media, the store hosts author readings, book clubs, and neighborhood events. They also send out a monthly printed newsletter to their most loyal customers. "Our customers don't just buy from us—they feel like they're part of something," says the owner. "That connection is something no algorithm can replicate."

Offline-first marketing isn't about abandoning digital tools entirely. It's about rebalancing the scales. By investing in strategies that foster genuine human connection, businesses can create a loyal customer base that isn't subject to the whims of a platform's latest update.

Why Small Businesses Must Adapt

For small businesses, the stakes are especially high. Unlike larger corporations, they don't have the resources to constantly adapt to algorithmic changes or outspend competitors on ads. Algorithm fatigue isn't just an annoyance—it's a threat to their survival.

But there's hope. Offline-first marketing offers a path forward that's not only more sustainable but also more rewarding. Here's why it matters:

First, it builds deeper connections. A handwritten thank-you note or a face-to-face conversation at a local event creates a lasting impression that a fleeting Instagram like never will.

Second, it's more predictable. Unlike social media, where reach can vanish overnight, offline strategies like direct mail or community partnerships deliver consistent results.

Finally, it's a differentiator. In a world where everyone is chasing viral moments, businesses that focus on real-world engagement stand out.

So where should small businesses start? Here are a few practical steps:

1. Host a local event. Whether it's a workshop, pop-up, or meetup, in-person gatherings are a powerful way to connect with your community.

2. Invest in print. A well-designed postcard or newsletter can cut through the digital noise.
3. Partner with other businesses. Collaborations can expand your reach without relying on ads.

Algorithm fatigue is more than just a buzzword—it's a wake-up call. For small businesses, the over-reliance on social media has become a risky bet in an increasingly unpredictable game. But by embracing offline-first marketing, they can reclaim control, build meaningful relationships, and create a brand that thrives beyond the scroll.

The age of algorithm fatigue doesn't have to be the end of growth. It can be the beginning of something better: a return to authenticity, connection, and marketing that truly serves both businesses and their customers. The choice is yours. Will you keep chasing the algorithm, or will you build something that lasts?

2

The Fundamentals of Offline-First Marketing

In an era dominated by digital noise, small business owners face an uphill battle: how to stand out when everyone is shouting into the same algorithmic void. Social media platforms promise reach and engagement, but the reality is often frustration—shrinking organic visibility, ever-changing algorithms, and a sense that your brand is just another drop in an endless digital ocean. There's a better way. Offline-First Marketing isn't about rejecting technology; it's about recentering your strategy around tangible, human connections that digital platforms can't replicate. This chapter will guide you through the principles, benefits, and practical steps to build a brand that thrives beyond the scroll.

What is Offline-First Marketing?

Offline-First Marketing is a strategy that prioritizes physical engagement, print media, and local community building over digital platforms. Unlike traditional marketing, which often treats offline efforts as secondary to digital campaigns, this approach flips the script. It recognizes that face-to-face interactions, tactile materials, and local presence create deeper, more lasting impressions than fleeting social media likes.

Consider the success of brands like Moo, the print design company that built its reputation on high-quality business cards and stationery.

By focusing on the tactile experience of their products, they turned customers into brand ambassadors—people who didn't just interact with Moo online but carried and shared their materials in the real world. Another example is the resurgence of independent bookstores, which have thrived by hosting author readings, book clubs, and community events rather than relying solely on online sales.

A common misconception is that offline marketing is outdated or less measurable than digital campaigns. In reality, tools like QR codes on print materials, event attendance tracking, and customer surveys provide robust data. The key difference? Offline efforts create memories, not just metrics.

Core Principles of Offline Marketing

Authenticity, consistency, and experiential value form the foundation of effective offline marketing. These principles ensure your efforts resonate deeply with your audience.

Authenticity means showing up as your brand's true self. A local coffee shop that handwrites thank-you notes to regulars builds more loyalty than a chain with a polished Instagram feed. Consistency is about creating reliable touchpoints—whether it's a monthly newsletter, a well-designed storefront, or a recurring community event. Experiential value transforms passive consumers into active participants. Think of a bakery offering free cookie-decorating workshops or a hardware store hosting DIY tutorials. These experiences forge emotional connections that no ad campaign can match.

To put these principles into action, start small. Design eye-catching business cards or flyers with a clear call to action. Partner with neighboring businesses for cross-promotions. Host a pop-up event to showcase your products in person. The goal isn't to abandon digital tools but to use them in service of real-world connections—for instance, promoting an in-person event through email invites rather than relying on social media algorithms to deliver your message.

The Benefits of Offline Marketing Over Social Media

The advantages of Offline-First Marketing are both practical and profound. First, it reduces dependency on algorithms. When your brand lives in the physical world—through print materials, events, or word-of-mouth—you're not at the mercy of a platform's ever-changing rules. Second, it fosters deeper relationships. A study by the Journal of Consumer Research found that face-to-face interactions increase trust and loyalty far more than digital exchanges. Third, it differentiates your brand. In a sea of sameness, a handwritten note or a well-curated in-store experience stands out.

Take the case of a small clothing boutique that shifted its focus from Instagram to local fashion shows and trunk sales. Not only did foot traffic increase, but customers spent more time in the store and developed personal relationships with the staff. Another example is a landscaper who replaced Facebook ads with beautifully designed brochures left at community centers. The tangible piece stayed in prospects' hands long after a digital ad would have been forgotten.

Practical Steps to Implement Offline-First Marketing

Transitioning to Offline-First Marketing doesn't require a massive budget—just intentionality. Begin by auditing your current efforts. What digital strategies are underperforming? Where could real-world interactions make a bigger impact?

Next, invest in high-quality print materials. Business cards, postcards, and brochures should reflect your brand's aesthetic and values.

Use them strategically: leave stacks at complementary local businesses, include them in orders, or hand them out at community events.

Host or participate in local events. A yoga studio might offer free classes in the park; a bakery could sponsor a neighborhood bake-off. These initiatives position your brand as a community pillar, not just a transactional entity.

Finally, build partnerships. Collaborate with other small businesses on joint promotions or events. A bookstore and a coffee shop might team up for a "Books and Brews" evening, driving traffic to both.

Common Pitfalls and How to Avoid Them

Even the best strategies can stumble without careful planning. One major pitfall is underestimating costs. While offline marketing can be cost-effective, quality matters—cheaply designed flyers or poorly planned events can hurt your brand. Budget for professionalism in print and execution.

Another mistake is failing to track ROI. Use unique promo codes, event sign-in sheets, or customer feedback forms to measure impact. Finally, don't neglect the follow-up. Collect contact information at events and follow up with personalized messages to nurture leads.

Offline-First Marketing isn't a rejection of the digital world; it's a reclamation of what makes your brand uniquely human. By prioritizing authenticity, consistency, and experiential value, you create connections that algorithms can't disrupt. Start small, stay intentional, and watch as your brand becomes a tangible presence in your customers' lives—not just another pixel on a screen. In the next chapter, we'll explore how to craft a compelling brand story that resonates both offline and on. But for now, take the first step: put down the phone, pick up a pen, and start building something real.

3

Getting Started: Setting Your Offline Goals

In a world dominated by digital noise, building a cult brand without social media might seem counterintuitive. Yet, some of the most enduring brands have thrived by fostering deep, real-world connections. This chapter will guide you through setting clear, actionable goals for growing your brand offline. We'll explore how to identify your audience, craft realistic objectives, and measure success—all without relying on algorithms or hashtags.

Understanding Your Audience Offline

The foundation of any successful brand is a deep understanding of its audience. Without social media analytics, how do you uncover who your ideal customers are? The answer lies in real-world engagement.

Start by immersing yourself in local events—farmers' markets, trade shows, or community gatherings—where your potential customers congregate. Observe their behaviors, listen to their conversations, and take note of their preferences. Face-to-face interactions provide insights no online survey can match.

Another powerful method is conducting in-person surveys. Set up a booth at a local fair or partner with a nearby café to gather feedback.

Ask open-ended questions: What problems do they face? What brands do they love? How do they discover new products? This qualitative data will help you craft customer personas grounded in real interactions.

Print media also offers a wealth of audience insights. If you run ads in local newspapers or magazines, track responses through dedicated phone lines or QR codes leading to a simple landing page. Pay attention to which messages resonate most. Over time, patterns will emerge, allowing you to refine your brand's voice and offerings.

Crafting Realistic Offline Goals

Once you understand your audience, the next step is setting goals that align with your brand's values and resources. Offline marketing requires a different approach than digital campaigns—it's slower, more deliberate, and often more personal.

SMART goals (Specific, Measurable, Achievable, Relevant, Time-bound) are just as valuable offline as they are online. For example, instead of aiming to "increase brand awareness," set a goal like, "Host three pop-up events in the next six months, each attracting at least 50 attendees." This specificity keeps you accountable and makes progress tangible.

Consider your brand's unique strengths. If you're a bakery, your goal might involve distributing 500 samples at a local festival and collecting email sign-ups from 30% of tasters. If you're a boutique, you could aim to partner with two complementary local businesses for cross-promotions within the next quarter.

Remember, offline goals should be rooted in community needs. If your town lacks a creative workshop space, hosting monthly DIY classes could position your brand as a local hub. Aligning your goals with community gaps not only builds loyalty but also ensures your efforts are meaningful.

Measuring Offline Success

Tracking offline success requires creativity, but it's far from impossible. Start with event metrics: attendance numbers, sign-ups for your mailing list, or the amount of product samples distributed. These hard numbers provide a baseline for engagement.

Feedback forms are another invaluable tool. Keep them simple—ask attendees to rate their experience on a scale of 1-5 and leave a brief comment. Look for recurring themes in their responses. Are people raving about your product's quality? Do they mention the welcoming atmosphere? This qualitative feedback is gold for refining future events.

For print campaigns, use trackable elements like coupon codes or unique URLs. If you place an ad in a local magazine, include a discount code specific to that publication. Monitor redemption rates to gauge the ad's effectiveness. Similarly, if you distribute flyers, use a dedicated phone number or landing page to track responses.

Don't underestimate the power of anecdotal evidence. A customer who stops by your store and mentions your recent newspaper feature is a sign your efforts are working. Encourage word-of-mouth by asking customers how they heard about you—over time, these stories will reveal which offline strategies are most impactful.

Case Studies: Offline Success Stories

To illustrate these principles, let's look at two small businesses that built cult brands without social media.

First, consider The Rustic Spoon, a family-owned restaurant in a mid-sized town. Instead of chasing Instagram fame, the owners focused on hosting monthly community dinners where locals could share stories over home-cooked meals. They tracked success through reservation numbers and repeat customers. Within a year, their dinners were consistently sold out, and their brand became synonymous with warmth and connection.

Another example is Inkwell Books, an independent bookstore that thrived by curating personalized reading recommendations. The owner set a goal to host one author reading and two book clubs per quarter, each attracting at least 20 attendees. By collecting feedback forms and tracking book sales tied to events, they refined their offerings and built a devoted following. Their secret? They prioritized depth over breadth, fostering a tight-knit community of book lovers.

These stories highlight a common thread: offline success comes from consistency, authenticity, and a willingness to listen.

Building a cult brand without social media isn't about rejecting technology—it's about reclaiming the human connections that make brands unforgettable. By understanding your audience through real-world interactions, setting SMART goals tailored to offline strategies, and creatively measuring success, you can create a brand that resonates deeply with your community.

The journey may be slower, but the rewards—loyal customers, meaningful relationships, and a brand that stands the test of time—are worth it. In the next chapter, we'll explore how to craft an offline marketing plan that brings these goals to life. For now, take the first step: step away from the screen, and step into your community.

4

Building Your Brand Identity Offline

In a world dominated by digital noise, the most memorable brands often stand out by embracing the tangible. While social media platforms come and go, the power of a well-crafted offline brand identity endures. This chapter will guide you through the process of creating a cohesive and compelling brand presence that thrives beyond the screen. From storytelling to visual design, we'll explore how to make your brand unforgettable in the real world.

The Power of a Compelling Brand Story

Every great brand is built on a story—one that resonates deeply with its audience. Your brand story isn't just a marketing tool; it's the emotional core of your business. To craft a narrative that sticks, start by identifying your core values, mission, and unique selling proposition. Ask yourself: Why does your business exist? What problem do you solve? How do you want customers to feel when they interact with your brand?

Once you've defined these elements, translate them into a narrative that can be shared offline. For example, a local coffee shop might center its story around community, sustainability, and the art of slow living. This narrative can then be communicated through face-to-face interactions, printed materials like menus or loyalty cards, and even the ambiance of the physical space.

A powerful brand story also thrives on authenticity. Avoid generic messaging—customers can spot insincerity from a mile away. Instead, lean into what makes your business unique. If your brand has humble beginnings, share that journey. If your products are handmade, highlight the craftsmanship. These details create emotional connections that digital ads alone can't replicate.

Designing Your Visual Identity for Print

Your visual identity is the face of your brand in the physical world. Unlike digital platforms, where designs can be tweaked instantly, print materials require careful planning to ensure consistency and impact. Start with the basics: logo, color palette, and typography. These elements should reflect your brand's personality and be versatile enough to work across various mediums.

Color theory plays a crucial role here. Colors evoke emotions—blue conveys trust, red energizes, green suggests sustainability. Choose a palette that aligns with your brand story and resonates with your audience. Similarly, typography should be legible and reflective of your brand's tone. A playful bakery might opt for rounded, friendly fonts, while a law firm would lean toward clean, professional serifs.

When designing for print, simplicity is key. Business cards, brochures, and packaging should be visually appealing but not cluttered. Work with a professional designer if possible, or use high-quality templates to maintain a polished look. Remember, print materials often serve as a customer's first impression of your brand—make it count.

Print Media as a Branding Tool

Print media offers a tactile experience that digital simply can't match. A well-designed flyer, catalog, or postcard can linger in a customer's hands long after they've scrolled past a social media post. The key is to choose the right materials for your business and distribute them strategically.

For example, a boutique clothing store might use beautifully printed lookbooks to showcase seasonal collections, while a restaurant could distribute branded coasters or napkins to reinforce its identity. Even small touches, like custom stickers or thank-you notes, can leave a lasting impression.

Print also excels at bridging the gap between online and offline. QR codes on posters can drive traffic to your website, while event programs can include social media handles to encourage digital engagement. The goal is to create a seamless brand experience, no matter where the customer encounters you.

Maintaining Consistency Across Offline Channels

Consistency is the backbone of brand recognition. Whether a customer sees your logo on a storefront, a business card, or a product label, they should instantly know it's you. To achieve this, develop a brand style guide that outlines your visual and verbal identity. Include guidelines for logo usage, color codes, fonts, and even tone of voice.

Train your team to embody your brand values in every interaction. From how they greet customers to the language they use in emails, these details reinforce your identity. Physical spaces, like your store or office, should also reflect your brand. Consider everything from signage to decor to the music playing in the background.

A simple but effective tool is a brand consistency checklist. Before launching any offline material, ask: Does this align with our colors and fonts? Is the messaging on-brand? Does it feel like us? Regular audits of your offline touchpoints can help catch inconsistencies before they confuse your audience.

Case Studies: Offline-First Brands That Nailed It

Some of the most iconic brands built their identities without relying on social media. Take Moleskine, for example. The notebook company cultivated a cult following by associating its products with creativity and legacy. Their minimalist design and strategic placement in bookstores and art supply shops made them a must-have for writers and artists.

On a smaller scale, consider a local bookstore that hosts author readings and community events. By creating a space where people can connect over shared interests, the store becomes more than a retailer—it becomes a cultural hub. Its handwritten shelf tags, curated book displays, and cozy seating all reinforce its brand as a haven for book lovers.

Another standout is Patagonia, whose commitment to environmental activism is woven into every aspect of its offline presence. From the recycled materials in its products to the grassroots events it sponsors, the brand's identity is unmistakable and deeply resonant.

Building a strong offline brand identity isn't about rejecting the digital world—it's about creating a holistic presence that thrives in both realms. By crafting a compelling story, designing a cohesive visual identity, leveraging print media, and maintaining consistency, you can build a brand that customers remember and trust.

The offline world offers something digital can't: tangibility, authenticity, and real human connection. In the next chapter, we'll explore how to amplify these efforts through community engagement and local partnerships. For now, take a moment to assess your current offline branding. Does it tell your story? Does it leave a lasting impression? If not, it's time to start rewriting the narrative—one printed page, one handshake, and one real-world interaction at a time.

5

Creating Memorable Real-World Events

In a world saturated with digital noise, real-world events stand out as a powerful way to connect with people on a deeper, more personal level. For small business owners, hosting an event isn't just about gathering a crowd—it's about creating an experience that leaves a lasting impression, builds trust, and fosters loyalty. Unlike social media, where algorithms dictate reach and engagement, events offer a unique opportunity to engage directly with your audience in a meaningful way. This chapter will guide you through the process of planning, executing, and leveraging events to amplify your brand without relying on digital platforms.

The Essentials of Event Planning

Successful events begin with thoughtful planning. The first step is to define your goals. Are you looking to increase brand awareness, foster community, or drive sales? Clear objectives will shape every decision, from the event format to the guest list. For example, if your goal is to build community, you might prioritize interactive workshops over formal presentations.

Next, consider your audience. Who are they, and what kind of experience would resonate with them? A small bookstore might host an intimate author reading for literary enthusiasts, while a fitness studio could organize a community workout in a local park. Aligning your event with your audience's interests ensures it feels relevant and engaging.

Choosing the right venue is equally critical. The space should reflect your brand's identity and accommodate your event's needs. A cozy café might be perfect for a knitting club meetup, but a larger space would be necessary for a product launch. Don't forget to factor in accessibility—ensuring everyone can comfortably attend is key to inclusivity.

Budgeting is another essential aspect of planning. Be realistic about what you can afford, and prioritize expenses that will enhance the attendee experience. Allocate funds for essentials like catering, décor, and marketing, but don't overlook smaller touches that can make a big impact, such as personalized name tags or branded swag.

Finally, create a detailed timeline to keep everything on track. Break down tasks into manageable steps, from booking vendors to sending invitations. A well-organized plan ensures smooth execution and reduces last-minute stress.

Designing Engaging Experiences

An event isn't just about gathering people in one place—it's about creating an experience that leaves a lasting impression. Start by thinking about how to immerse attendees in your brand's story. For example, a boutique tea company could host a tea-tasting event where participants learn about the origins and cultural significance of each blend. This not only educates but also builds a deeper connection to the product.

Interactive elements are key to engagement. Hands-on activities, Q&A sessions, or live demonstrations invite participation and make the event feel dynamic. A craft brewery might offer a behind-the-scenes tour followed by a DIY beer-crafting session, giving attendees a hands-on experience they'll remember.

Storytelling is another powerful tool. Use narratives to convey your brand's mission and values. Share the story of how your business started, or highlight the impact you've made in the community. Stories humanize your brand and create emotional resonance.

Personalization can elevate the experience. Greet attendees by name, offer tailored recommendations, or provide opportunities for them to share their own stories. A skincare brand, for instance, could offer one-on-one consultations to help guests find products that suit their needs.

Remember, subtlety is key when incorporating brand messaging. The goal is to create an authentic experience, not a sales pitch. Focus on adding value and fostering connections, and the rest will follow.

Building Community During the Event

Events are a unique opportunity to bring people together and foster a sense of community. Start by creating an inclusive atmosphere where everyone feels welcome. Clear signage, friendly staff, and thoughtful touches like name tags can help attendees feel at ease.

Facilitate connections among attendees by encouraging networking. Icebreaker activities, shared experiences, or designated conversation areas can help people mingle naturally. For example, a co-working space might organize a networking breakfast where members can share ideas and collaborate.

Shared experiences are another powerful way to build community. Group activities, such as a cooking class or a volunteer project, create a sense of camaraderie and leave attendees with lasting memories. These moments not only strengthen bonds among attendees but also deepen their connection to your brand.

Don't underestimate the power of inclusivity. Ensure your event is accessible to all, regardless of physical ability, language, or cultural background. Providing accommodations like sign language interpreters, multilingual materials, or dietary options demonstrates your commitment to inclusivity and enhances the overall experience.

Finally, make attendees feel valued. Express genuine gratitude for their presence, listen to their feedback, and show interest in their stories. When people feel appreciated, they're more likely to become loyal advocates for your brand.

Post-Event Follow-Up and Amplification

The impact of your event doesn't end when the last guest leaves. Follow-up is crucial for maintaining momentum and converting attendees into long-term supporters. Start by gathering feedback. Surveys, informal conversations, or social media polls can provide insights into what worked well and what could be improved. Use this feedback to refine future events.

Send personalized thank-you notes to attendees. A heartfelt email, handwritten card, or small token of appreciation shows you value their involvement. Include a call to action, such as joining your mailing list, following your blog, or attending your next event.

Leverage event-generated content to extend its reach. Share photos, videos, or testimonials from the event on your print materials, website, or newsletter. Highlighting the positive experiences of attendees not only reinforces their memories but also attracts new interest.

Maintain momentum by staying connected. Follow up with attendees through regular updates, exclusive offers, or invitations to upcoming events. Keep the lines of communication open and continue to add value to their lives.

Finally, reflect on the event's success. Did you achieve your goals? What lessons did you learn? Use this reflection to inform future strategies and continue building your brand through real-world connections.

Real-world events are more than just marketing tools—they are opportunities to create meaningful, memorable experiences that resonate deeply with your audience. By aligning your event with your brand's values and your audience's needs, designing engaging experiences, fostering community, and extending the impact through thoughtful follow-up, you can build a loyal following without relying on social media. In a world where digital interactions often feel impersonal, events remind us of the power of human connection. Embrace this opportunity to bring your brand to life and leave a lasting impression on everyone who walks through your door.

6

Leveraging Print Media for Brand Awareness

In an era dominated by digital noise, small business owners often find themselves grappling with algorithm fatigue, dwindling engagement, and the fleeting nature of online content. Amidst this chaos, print media emerges as a refreshingly tangible, trustworthy, and enduring medium for building brand awareness. Unlike the ephemeral scroll of social media, print materials offer a lasting presence that engages audiences on a deeper, sensory level. This chapter explores how small business owners can harness the power of print media to cultivate a cult brand, from designing impactful materials to strategically distributing them and measuring their success.

The Power of Print: Why Tangible Media Still Matters

In a world saturated with digital ads, print media stands out for its permanence and credibility. Studies consistently show that consumers perceive print materials as more trustworthy than digital content. According to a 2022 study by Two Sides North America, 74% of consumers trust print advertisements more than online ads. This trust stems from the tactile nature of print, which engages multiple senses and creates a memorable impression.

Print media also benefits from its staying power. A brochure left on a coffee table or a poster hung in a community space continues to influence long after a social media post disappears from a feed. This durability makes print an ideal medium for building brand loyalty. For example, the skincare brand Glossier initially gained popularity through its beautifully designed print catalogs, which not only showcased products but also conveyed the brand's ethos in a way that resonated deeply with customers.

By leveraging print media, small businesses can differentiate themselves, foster trust, and create a lasting connection with their audience. In a crowded digital landscape, print offers a unique opportunity to stand out and make a meaningful impact.

Designing Print Materials that Resonate

The effectiveness of print media hinges on its design. Visually compelling materials capture attention, communicate your brand's story, and leave a lasting impression. To create print materials that resonate, start by selecting the right format. Brochures, postcards, posters, and flyers each serve different purposes and audiences. For instance, a brochure is ideal for detailed product information, while a postcard works well for concise, eye-catching promotions.

Next, focus on high-quality imagery and typography. Your visuals should reflect your brand's personality and values. Invest in professional photography or illustrations that align with your aesthetic. Typography also plays a crucial role in readability and brand identity. Choose fonts that are clean and legible while maintaining a distinctive style.

Messaging is equally important. In print, brevity is key. Craft concise, persuasive text that communicates your value proposition clearly. Use headlines to grab attention and body text to provide essential details. For example, the outdoor apparel brand Patagonia excels at storytelling through its catalogues, using powerful imagery and minimalist text to convey its commitment to sustainability.

Finally, don't overlook the importance of physical quality. High-quality paper, finishes, and printing techniques enhance the perceived value of your materials, reinforcing your brand's credibility.

Strategic Distribution: Getting Your Materials in Front of the Right People

Designing exceptional print materials is only half the battle; ensuring they reach the right audience is equally critical. Strategic distribution maximizes the impact of your efforts while minimizing costs. One effective method is direct mail, which allows you to target specific demographics based on geographic data or customer profiles. For instance, a local coffee shop could send postcards to households within a five-mile radius, offering a discount on their first visit.

Partnering with local businesses and community organizations can also amplify your reach. Collaborate with complementary brands to distribute materials in their stores or event spaces. For example, a yoga studio might partner with a health food store to share brochures or posters.

Event giveaways are another powerful distribution strategy. Attend industry conventions, farmers' markets, or community events to hand out flyers, brochures, or branded merchandise. This not only increases visibility but also creates opportunities for face-to-face interactions with potential customers.

A case study that illustrates the power of strategic distribution comes from the small bakery "Sweet Temptations." By placing beautifully designed postcards in nearby cafes and mailing them to local households, the bakery saw a 30% increase in foot traffic within three months.

Measuring Success: How to Track and Optimize Your Print Campaigns

To justify the investment in print media, it's essential to measure its impact and optimize future efforts. One effective tracking method is the use of QR codes or custom URLs on your materials. These tools allow you to monitor engagement by tracking how many people visit your website or landing page after interacting with your print materials.

Customer surveys are another valuable tool for gauging the effectiveness of your campaigns. Include questions about how customers discovered your business and which materials influenced their decision. This feedback provides insights into which distribution methods are most effective.

Analyzing sales data can also help quantify the ROI of your print campaigns. Compare sales trends before and after distributing materials to identify correlations. For example, if you notice a spike in sales of a specific product after mailing a brochure featuring it, you can attribute this success to your print efforts.

Finally, use the data you collect to refine future campaigns. Identify which designs, messaging, and distribution methods yield the best results and replicate these strategies moving forward.

Integrating Print Media into Your Overall Marketing Strategy

Print media should not operate in isolation; it works best when integrated with other marketing channels. A cohesive brand experience requires consistent messaging and visuals across all touchpoints. Start by aligning your print materials with your digital presence. For example, use the same color palette, imagery, and tone of voice in your brochures, website, and social media posts.

Next, create a marketing plan that balances print and digital efforts. Allocate resources based on your target audience's preferences and behaviors. For instance, if your audience skews older, prioritize direct mail campaigns. For younger audiences, complement print materials with social media ads or email newsletters.

Timing is also crucial. Coordinate print and digital campaigns to reinforce each other. Launch a direct mail campaign simultaneously with a social media campaign to create multiple touchpoints that drive home your message.

Finally, evaluate the effectiveness of your integrated marketing strategy regularly. Use the tracking methods discussed earlier to assess how each channel contributes to your overall goals and adjust your approach as needed.

In a world overwhelmed by digital clutter, print media offers small businesses a powerful tool for building brand awareness and fostering deeper connections with their audience. By designing visually compelling materials, distributing them strategically, and measuring their impact, small business owners can harness the enduring power of print to create a cult brand without relying on social media. Print media's tangibility, credibility, and sensory engagement make it a valuable addition to any marketing strategy, providing a refreshing alternative to the fleeting nature of digital content. As you integrate print into your overall marketing efforts, remember that consistency and creativity are key to creating a lasting impression that resonates with your audience.

7

The Power of Local Community Engagement

In today's fast-paced, digital-first world, it's easy to overlook the profound impact of offline, community-centered strategies. Yet, as small business owners, tapping into the power of local community engagement can be transformative. It's not just about building a customer base; it's about embedding your brand within the fabric of your community, fostering trust, and creating relationships that endure. This chapter explores how focusing on local partnerships, workshops, and authentic support can help you cultivate a cult brand that thrives independently of social media's unpredictable algorithms. Let's dive into why local engagement matters and how you can harness its potential.

Why Local Community Engagement Matters

Social media has become the default marketing strategy for many businesses, but its shortcomings are increasingly apparent. Algorithms change frequently, organic reach is limited, and the online space is saturated with competition. While digital platforms can be useful tools, relying on them exclusively often leaves businesses feeling disconnected from their core audience. Local community engagement, on the other hand, offers a way to build trust and loyalty by meeting people where they are—literally.

When you engage with your local community, you're not just selling a product or service; you're becoming a part of people's lives. Your brand becomes associated with shared experiences, meaningful interactions, and a sense of belonging. This is especially important for small businesses, which often rely on repeat customers and word-of-mouth referrals. By focusing on local engagement, you create a sustainable marketing ecosystem that doesn't hinge on the whims of social media trends.

Consider the example of a small bakery that hosts monthly cookie decorating workshops for local families. Not only does this activity draw customers into the store, but it also creates a memorable experience that fosters loyalty. Families return not just for the cookies but for the sense of community they've found. This kind of connection is difficult to replicate online.

Partnering with Local Businesses: Collaboration Over Competition

One of the most effective ways to engage with your local community is through partnerships with neighboring businesses. Collaboration over competition can amplify your reach, create unique value for customers, and foster a supportive local ecosystem. The key is to identify businesses that complement your own, rather than viewing them as rivals.

For instance, a boutique clothing store might partner with a local jewelry maker to co-host a "Fashion Night Out" event. Customers could enjoy discounts at both stores, participate in a style workshop, and even enter a raffle for a gift basket featuring products from both businesses. This type of collaboration provides added value for customers and introduces each business to the other's audience.

To start, create a list of local businesses that align with your brand's values and target audience. Reach out with a collaborative mindset, emphasizing the mutual benefits of working together. Co-hosting events, cross-promotions, and joint initiatives are just a few ways to build these partnerships. Remember, the goal isn't just to increase sales—it's to create a sense of unity within the community.

A real-world example of this strategy is the partnership between a coffee shop and a nearby bookstore. Together, they launched a "Book and Brew" series, where customers could enjoy a discounted coffee while attending book signings or literary discussions. The collaboration not only drove foot traffic to both businesses but also positioned them as cultural hubs within the community.

Hosting Community Workshops: Educate, Engage, and Empower

Workshops are a powerful tool for educating, engaging, and empowering your community. They allow you to share your expertise while creating a space for meaningful interaction. Whether you're a florist teaching a flower arrangement class or a tech store hosting a smartphone photography workshop, these events can deepen your connection with your audience.

The first step is to choose a topic that resonates with your community's interests and aligns with your brand. For example, a fitness studio might host a free yoga class in the park, while a craft store could offer a DIY candle-making workshop. The key is to provide value that goes beyond transactional benefits.

Once you've chosen a topic, focus on creating a memorable experience. Use offline marketing methods like flyers, posters, and word-of-mouth to spread the word. During the event, prioritize interaction and engagement. Encourage participants to ask questions, share their experiences, and connect with one another. This fosters a sense of community that extends beyond the workshop itself.

A practical example of this is a small gardening center that hosted a "Native Plants for Urban Gardens" workshop. Attendees learned about sustainable gardening practices while getting hands-on experience planting their own seedlings. The workshop not only increased awareness of the gardening center's offerings but also positioned it as a resource for eco-conscious living.

Building Loyalty Through Local Support: Give Before You Receive

One of the most profound ways to build loyalty within your community is by demonstrating genuine care and support. This means prioritizing the needs of your community and giving back in meaningful ways. Whether it's sponsoring local events, donating to causes, or offering free services, these actions create goodwill that translates into customer loyalty.

Sponsoring local events, such as a school fundraiser or a neighborhood clean-up, is a great way to show your commitment to the community. It positions your brand as a local leader and introduces you to potential customers in a positive light. Donating to causes that align with your values, such as supporting a local food bank or animal shelter, further cements your reputation as a business that cares.

Offering free services or products can also make a significant impact. For example, a hair salon might provide free haircuts for children before the school year starts, or a restaurant could host a free community dinner. These gestures build trust and create a lasting impression that encourages customers to support your business in return.

A notable example is a small printing shop that offered free marketing materials for local nonprofits. Not only did this help the nonprofits achieve their goals, but it also attracted new customers who admired the shop's generosity. Over time, this commitment to local support turned customers into lifelong advocates.

Local community engagement is more than just a marketing strategy—it's a way to build a brand rooted in trust, loyalty, and authentic connection. By partnering with neighboring businesses, hosting community workshops, and demonstrating genuine support, you can create a sustainable marketing ecosystem that thrives independently of social media. These strategies not only foster a sense of belonging but also position your business as a cornerstone of your community.

As you implement these ideas, remember that local engagement is a long-term investment. The relationships you build today will yield dividends for years to come, transforming your business into a cult brand that customers feel proud to support. In a world increasingly dominated by digital noise, the power of local community engagement offers a refreshing and deeply human alternative. Embrace it, and watch your business flourish.

8

Analog Connection: The Human Touch

In an era where digital interactions dominate, the power of analog connection remains an untapped superpower for small businesses. While social media and email campaigns have their place, the brands that truly stand out are those that prioritize the human touch. This chapter explores how personalized, offline-first strategies can create deeper customer relationships, foster loyalty, and set your brand apart in an oversaturated digital landscape.

The Power of Personalization

Personalization is more than just addressing a customer by name—it's about making them feel seen and valued. Research shows that 80% of consumers are more likely to purchase from a brand that offers personalized experiences. For small businesses, this doesn't require complex algorithms or expensive software. It starts with simple, intentional actions.

One effective method is remembering customer preferences. A local coffee shop owner might note that a regular orders a vanilla latte every Tuesday and surprise them with a free upgrade on their next visit. A boutique clothing store could keep track of a client's favorite colors and send a message when new arrivals match their taste. These small gestures demonstrate attentiveness and build emotional connections.

Another strategy is customized recommendations. Instead of generic promotions, tailor suggestions based on past purchases. For example, a bookstore owner who knows a customer loves historical fiction might handpick a new release and include a handwritten note explaining why they thought of them. This level of personalization transforms a transaction into a meaningful interaction.

Handwritten Notes: A Lost Art

In a world of automated emails and templated messages, handwritten notes stand out as a rare and powerful tool. They convey effort, thoughtfulness, and authenticity—qualities that digital communication often lacks. Studies indicate that handwritten notes are 10 times more likely to be remembered than digital ones, making them a high-impact, low-cost marketing strategy.

The key to effective handwritten notes lies in their timing and content. A thank-you note sent immediately after a purchase reinforces gratitude, while a follow-up note a few weeks later checks in on the customer's satisfaction. The tone should be warm and personal, avoiding salesy language. For instance, a florist might write, "We loved creating the bouquet for your anniversary—hope it brought joy to your celebration!"

Case studies reveal the tangible benefits of this approach. A skincare brand that included handwritten thank-you notes with every order saw a 25% increase in repeat customers within six months. A real estate agent who sent personalized notes to clients after closings reported higher referral rates. These examples prove that small investments in analog communication yield significant returns.

Building Lasting Impressions

Beyond handwritten notes, small gestures can leave indelible marks on customers. Follow-up calls, surprise gifts, and personalized thank-you packages demonstrate that your business values relationships over transactions. The key is consistency—these efforts should feel like a natural extension of your brand, not a one-off marketing tactic.

Consider the impact of a follow-up call after a service is rendered. A hair stylist might call a client two days after a major cut to ensure they're happy with the result. This not only builds trust but also opens the door for feedback and future bookings. Similarly, surprise gifts—like a complimentary sample or a discount on a future purchase—create delight and encourage loyalty.

Authenticity is crucial. Customers can spot performative gestures, so focus on sincerity. A bakery that includes a free cookie with a note saying, "Thanks for supporting our small business—enjoy a little treat on us!" feels genuine, while a generic corporate gift might fall flat.

Case Studies: Analog Success Stories

Several businesses have thrived by prioritizing analog connections. Take the example of a family-owned hardware store that implemented a "customer memory" system. Employees jot down details about regulars—like their home renovation projects or preferred tools—and reference them in future conversations. This practice led to a 40% increase in customer retention over two years.

Another success story comes from a stationery shop that sends handwritten birthday cards to its loyalty program members. Each card includes a small discount, but the personal touch—not the promotion—drives engagement. The shop's owner reports that customers often visit just to thank her for the card, turning a simple gesture into a sales opportunity.

These examples highlight a universal truth: people crave connection. In a digital age, businesses that deliver it authentically gain a competitive edge.

Avoiding Common Pitfalls

While analog strategies are powerful, they come with potential pitfalls. Overcommitting is a common mistake. Sending handwritten notes to every customer might be unsustainable as your business grows. Instead, focus on high-impact moments—first-time buyers, loyal clients, or post-purchase follow-ups.

Lack of authenticity is another risk. Customers can tell when gestures are robotic or insincere. Avoid pre-printed thank-you cards with no personalization. Even a short, genuine note trumps a generic message.

Inconsistency can also undermine your efforts. If you start with personalized follow-ups but abandon them after a few months, customers may feel undervalued. Choose strategies you can maintain long-term, even if they're modest in scale.

In a world where digital noise is constant, analog connections offer a refreshing and impactful alternative. Personalized interactions, handwritten notes, and thoughtful gestures create emotional bonds that algorithms cannot replicate. For small business owners, these strategies are not just nostalgic—they're a proven way to build a cult brand that customers love and advocate for.

The human touch is your secret weapon. Use it intentionally, authentically, and consistently, and watch your business thrive in ways no digital campaign could achieve.

9

Case Studies: Brands That Thrived Offline

In an era dominated by digital noise, some brands have chosen a different path—one that prioritizes real-world connections over virtual engagement. These businesses have built cult-like followings not through viral posts or influencer partnerships, but by fostering genuine relationships with their communities. This chapter explores three such brands that thrived by embracing offline-first strategies. Their stories reveal the power of face-to-face interactions, immersive experiences, and the kind of authenticity that algorithms can't replicate.

The brands we'll examine—a local bookstore, an artisanal bakery, and a fitness studio—each faced unique challenges in their early days. Yet, they all shared a common belief: that meaningful engagement happens in person. By focusing on offline tactics like community events, hands-on workshops, and exclusive in-person offerings, they cultivated loyal customer bases that sustained their growth. Their success offers valuable lessons for small business owners looking to break free from the scroll and connect with their audience in more impactful ways.

Case Study 1: The Local Bookstore Revival

When the digital age threatened to render independent bookstores obsolete, one small shop in a mid-sized city defied the odds. Instead of competing with online retailers on price or convenience, the store's owner, Sarah, doubled down on what she could offer that Amazon couldn't: a sense of belonging.

Sarah transformed her bookstore into a community hub by hosting weekly book clubs, author signings, and storytelling nights for children. She partnered with local schools to create reading challenges and even curated a "blind date with a book" display, where customers purchased wrapped books based on handwritten recommendations from staff. These efforts didn't just drive foot traffic—they created a tribe of devoted patrons who saw the store as a second home.

The key takeaway here is the power of creating a third place—a term sociologists use to describe spaces that aren't home or work but where people gather to connect. For Sarah's bookstore, this meant designing events that encouraged repeat visits and organic word-of-mouth marketing. Small business owners can replicate this by identifying what unique experiences their brand can offer and how to make their physical space a destination, not just a point of sale.

Case Study 2: The Artisanal Bakery Experience

In a crowded market of chain bakeries and grocery store desserts, one artisanal bakery stood out by making its customers feel like part of the process. The bakery's owner, Miguel, understood that people craved more than just a pastry—they wanted a story, a connection to the craft.

Miguel launched a series of in-person baking classes, where customers could learn to make his signature sourdough or decorate seasonal cupcakes. He also organized farm-to-table dinners, collaborating with local farmers to showcase the ingredients behind his creations. These events weren't just revenue streams; they were marketing tools that turned casual customers into brand advocates.

Perhaps the most innovative strategy was the bakery's pop-up shops at farmers' markets and neighborhood festivals. Instead of waiting for customers to come to him, Miguel brought his brand to them, offering samples and exclusive items only available at these events. This not only expanded his reach but also created a sense of urgency and exclusivity.

For small business owners, the lesson is clear: offline engagement can turn transactions into relationships. Whether it's workshops, pop-ups, or collaborative events, giving customers a hands-on experience with your product fosters loyalty and word-of-mouth buzz.

Case Study 3: The Fitness Studio Phenomenon

While fitness apps and on-demand workouts boomed, one local studio grew a devoted following by offering something screens couldn't: human energy. The studio's founder, Jamal, built his brand around the idea that fitness is as much about community as it is about exercise.

Jamal's studio offered exclusive in-person classes with limited spots, creating a sense of scarcity and prestige. He also organized weekend wellness retreats, where clients could bond over hikes, meditation sessions, and healthy meals. These retreats weren't just profitable; they deepened emotional connections to the brand.

Merchandise played a surprising role, too. The studio sold high-quality, branded apparel that became a status symbol in the local fitness scene. Wearing the studio's logo wasn't just about fashion—it signaled membership in an exclusive club.

The fitness studio's success underscores the importance of creating a unique, immersive experience. For small business owners, this means thinking beyond the product or service itself and considering how to make customers feel like they're part of something special.

Key Lessons and Takeaways

These three case studies reveal several common threads in successful offline-first branding. First, each brand prioritized creating a sense of community, whether through events, workshops, or exclusive offerings. Second, they all leveraged scarcity and exclusivity to drive demand—limited spots, pop-up shops, or one-of-a-kind experiences. Third, they understood that their physical spaces were more than transactional locations; they were stages for storytelling and connection.

Another critical takeaway is the role of word-of-mouth marketing. Offline strategies often generate organic buzz because they're memorable and shareable. A customer who attends a book club or a baking class is more likely to tell friends about it than someone who simply clicks an ad.

Applying the Lessons to Your Business

So, how can you translate these insights into action? Start by asking yourself: What unique experiences can my business offer that can't be replicated online? Here are a few practical steps to get started:

1. Identify your community's needs. Survey your customers or observe their behavior to understand what they value most.
2. Design events or experiences that align with your brand's mission. Whether it's a workshop, a meetup, or a limited-edition product, make it something worth talking about.
3. Leverage partnerships. Collaborate with other local businesses to co-host events or cross-promote, expanding your reach.

4. Create exclusivity. Offer VIP access, early-bird pricing, or members-only perks to foster a sense of belonging.

Finally, remember that offline strategies require patience. Unlike a viral post, the payoff may take time, but the relationships you build will be far more enduring.

The brands in this chapter prove that in a world obsessed with digital metrics, the most powerful marketing tool is still human connection. By focusing on offline-first strategies, they built loyal followings that no algorithm could dictate. For small business owners, the message is clear: step away from the screen and into the real world. Your customers are waiting.

10

Avoiding Common Pitfalls in Offline Marketing

Transitioning to an offline-first marketing strategy can feel like stepping into uncharted territory. For small business owners accustomed to the instant gratification and measurable metrics of social media campaigns, the shift requires a new mindset and a fresh set of skills. While offline marketing offers unique opportunities to connect with your audience in meaningful ways, it also comes with its own set of challenges. In this chapter, we'll explore the most common mistakes businesses make when moving away from digital platforms and provide actionable strategies to help you navigate these pitfalls with confidence.

Identifying Common Offline Marketing Mistakes

One of the first steps in avoiding mistakes is recognizing them. Offline marketing can be a powerful tool, but it's easy to stumble if you approach it without a clear plan. One frequent misstep is underestimating the costs involved. Unlike social media, where campaigns can be launched with minimal budgets, offline marketing often requires upfront investments in materials, events, or partnerships. Without proper budgeting, these expenses can quickly spiral out of control.

Another common error is failing to define clear goals. Offline campaigns require intention and focus. Without specific objectives—whether it's increasing foot traffic, boosting brand awareness, or generating leads—your efforts may lack direction and fail to deliver results. Additionally, overlooking audience targeting can lead to wasted resources. For example, a local bakery investing in a full-page newspaper ad might find that it doesn't resonate with their core customer base, who are more likely to engage with community events or word-of-mouth recommendations.

Real-world examples illustrate these pitfalls. Consider a small clothing boutique that spent thousands on billboard ads without researching whether their target demographic commuted on that route. The campaign failed to generate sales because it didn't align with their audience's habits. By identifying these mistakes early, you can avoid costly errors and set your offline marketing strategy on the right path.

Effective Resource Allocation for Offline Campaigns

Once you've identified potential pitfalls, the next step is to allocate your resources wisely. Offline marketing doesn't have to break the bank, but it does require thoughtful planning. Start by prioritizing cost-effective strategies that align with your goals. For instance, print media—such as flyers or postcards—can be a powerful tool when used strategically. Focus on high-traffic areas where your target audience is likely to be, such as local cafes, libraries, or community centers.

Event planning is another area where resource allocation is crucial. Hosting an event can be a great way to engage your community, but it's important to balance ambition with practicality. Start small with pop-up shops or workshops before scaling up to larger events. Collaborating with local businesses can also reduce costs while expanding your reach. For example, partnering with a nearby bookstore for a joint event allows you to share expenses and tap into each other's customer bases.

Maximizing ROI in offline marketing often comes down to creativity and planning. Consider how you can repurpose materials or leverage existing relationships to stretch your budget. A well-designed brochure, for example, can double as a handout at events and a mailing piece for direct outreach. By thinking strategically about your resources, you can make every dollar count.

Building Authentic Local Connections

One of the greatest advantages of offline marketing is the opportunity to foster genuine relationships within your community. These connections can drive loyalty and create a strong foundation for your brand. Begin by collaborating with local businesses and organizations. Mutual support strengthens the community while introducing your brand to new audiences. For example, a coffee shop might team up with a local artist to host a gallery night, creating a memorable experience that benefits both parties.

Hosting impactful events is another way to build authentic connections. Focus on providing value to your attendees rather than simply promoting your products. A cooking class, for instance, can attract food enthusiasts while subtly showcasing your kitchenware line. The key is to create experiences that resonate with your audience and leave a lasting impression.

Customer interactions also play a crucial role in building local relationships. Train your team to provide exceptional service and create moments that customers will remember. A simple gesture, like a handwritten thank-you note with a purchase, can make a lasting impact. By prioritizing authenticity and community engagement, you'll cultivate a loyal customer base that supports your brand long-term.

Measuring Success in Offline Marketing

Tracking the effectiveness of offline campaigns can be more challenging than digital efforts, but it's essential for understanding your ROI. Start by establishing clear metrics for success. For example, if you're hosting an event, measure attendance numbers, customer feedback, and any follow-up sales. Use tools like surveys or comment cards to gather insights directly from participants.

Sales data is another valuable indicator of campaign success. Compare sales trends before and after your offline efforts to gauge their impact. If you're running a print campaign, include unique codes or offers to track customer responses. For example, a coupon code specific to a flyer campaign can help you determine how many sales resulted from that initiative.

Remember that offline marketing often has a cumulative effect. While immediate results are important, consider the long-term benefits of increased brand awareness and customer loyalty. By combining quantitative data with qualitative feedback, you'll gain a comprehensive understanding of your campaign's effectiveness.

Long-Term Planning and Adaptability

Sustained success in offline marketing requires strategic planning and adaptability. Begin by setting long-term goals that align with your overall business vision. For example, if expanding your local presence is a priority, consider how offline campaigns can support that objective over time. Develop a roadmap that outlines your key initiatives, timelines, and resource needs.

Flexibility is equally important. Consumer behaviors and market conditions evolve, and your offline strategy must be able to adapt. Regularly review your campaigns' performance and be willing to pivot when necessary. For instance, if a particular event format isn't resonating with your audience, experiment with new approaches to see what works best.

Staying relevant in a changing landscape also means keeping an ear to the ground. Engage with your community to understand their needs and preferences. Attend local meetings, participate in neighborhood events, and listen to customer feedback. By staying connected and responsive, you'll ensure that your offline marketing efforts remain impactful and aligned with your audience's interests.

Transitioning to an offline-first marketing strategy is a journey filled with opportunities and challenges. By recognizing common pitfalls and equipping yourself with practical strategies, you can navigate this shift with confidence. Effective resource allocation, authentic local connections, and diligent measurement are the cornerstones of a successful offline campaign. Above all, long-term planning and adaptability will ensure that your efforts continue to resonate with your audience and drive sustained growth for your business. As you embark on this path, remember that offline marketing is not just about selling a product—it's about building a brand that thrives in the hearts and minds of your community.

11

Advanced Strategies for Offline Growth

In today's digital-saturated world, standing out requires more than just another social media post. Algorithm fatigue is real, and consumers are craving authentic, tangible connections with brands. This chapter is designed for small business owners ready to break free from the scroll and build lasting relationships through offline-first strategies. We'll explore how to scale your offline efforts, bridge the gap between physical and digital experiences, and implement innovative tactics that leave a lasting impression.

Maximizing Offline Campaigns at Scale

Scaling offline marketing doesn't mean sacrificing the personal touch that makes it so powerful. Instead, it's about expanding your reach while maintaining authenticity. Start by identifying which offline efforts already resonate with your audience—whether it's local events, print ads, or word-of-mouth referrals—and build from there.

One effective strategy is hosting larger-scale events. If your pop-up shop or workshop was a hit, consider partnering with a local venue to host a bigger version. Collaborate with complementary businesses to share costs and expand your audience. For example, a boutique clothing store might team up with a jewelry designer and a local café to create a curated shopping experience.

Print media remains a powerful tool for scaling offline efforts. While digital ads get lost in the noise, a well-designed postcard or magazine feature can linger in a customer's home for weeks. Invest in high-quality materials that reflect your brand's aesthetic, and distribute them in strategic locations—think coffee shops, coworking spaces, or community bulletin boards.

Measuring ROI is critical when scaling. Use unique promo codes, QR links, or dedicated landing pages to track how offline efforts drive sales or website traffic. Surveys and follow-up emails can also provide qualitative insights into customer sentiment. The key is to start small, test, and then expand what works.

Bridging Offline and Online Experiences

The most successful brands create a seamless journey between offline and online touchpoints. Your goal is to make it effortless for customers to move from a physical interaction to engaging with your digital presence—and vice versa.

QR codes are a simple yet effective bridge. Place them on business cards, product packaging, or event signage to direct customers to your website, a special offer, or even a behind-the-scenes video. For example, a bakery could include a QR code on their pastry boxes linking to a recipe blog or a loyalty program signup.

Hybrid events are another powerful way to merge offline and online. Host an in-person workshop while simultaneously live-streaming for remote attendees. Encourage participants to share their experiences on social media with a branded hashtag, creating organic online buzz. After the event, follow up with an email recap and exclusive content to keep the momentum going.

Don't overlook the power of offline interactions to fuel online engagement. Train your team to invite customers to join your email list or follow your social channels. A simple ask at checkout—"Want to stay updated on future events?"—can significantly grow your digital audience.

Innovative Offline Marketing Tactics

To truly stand out, think beyond traditional flyers and billboards. Guerrilla marketing—unexpected, creative campaigns that capture attention—can generate buzz without a hefty budget. For instance, a fitness brand might organize a flash mob workout in a public park, handing out branded water bottles to participants.

Pop-up experiences are another way to create memorable moments. A bookstore could set up a cozy reading nook in a busy downtown area, offering free coffee and book recommendations. These temporary installations not only attract foot traffic but also give customers a taste of your brand's personality.

Collaborations can amplify your reach. Partner with local artists to create limited-edition merchandise, or team up with influencers for a real-world meet-and-greet. These partnerships add credibility and introduce your brand to new audiences in an organic way.

Case Studies: Offline Success Stories

Real-world examples illustrate the power of offline strategies. Take the case of a small skincare brand that grew its customer base by hosting free skincare workshops at local yoga studios. Attendees received samples and personalized advice, leading to a 30% increase in repeat purchases. The brand also encouraged attendees to share their experiences online, creating a ripple effect of word-of-mouth referrals.

Another success story involves a coffee roastery that partnered with a regional magazine for a featured article. The piece included a tear-out coupon for a free drink, driving foot traffic to their café. By tracking coupon redemptions, they measured a clear ROI and built a loyal local following.

These examples highlight a common thread: offline efforts thrive when they're personal, experiential, and tied to measurable outcomes.

Avoiding Common Pitfalls in Offline Marketing

Even the best strategies can falter without careful planning. One major pitfall is underestimating costs. Offline campaigns often require upfront investment in materials, venues, or staffing. Create a detailed budget and start with low-cost pilots before committing to large-scale initiatives.

Another mistake is failing to align offline efforts with your overall brand. Every touchpoint—from event signage to packaging—should reflect your brand's voice and values. Inconsistency can confuse customers and dilute your message.

Finally, don't neglect follow-up. An amazing event or campaign means little if you don't nurture the relationships it creates. Collect contact information, send thank-you notes, and provide exclusive offers to keep customers engaged long after the interaction.

Offline growth isn't about rejecting digital tools—it's about creating a balanced, customer-centric approach that prioritizes real connections.

By scaling thoughtfully, bridging offline and online experiences, and embracing creativity, you can build a brand that thrives beyond the screen. The strategies in this chapter are your toolkit for turning fleeting interactions into lasting loyalty. Start small, stay authentic, and watch your community grow—one handshake, one event, one conversation at a time.

12

The Role of Customer Feedback in Offline Marketing

In an age dominated by social media algorithms and digital metrics, it's easy to overlook the profound value of direct, authentic customer feedback. For small businesses striving to build a cult brand without relying on social media, understanding and acting on customer insights is not just beneficial—it's essential. This chapter explores how offline marketing strategies can be significantly enhanced by leveraging customer feedback. We'll discuss why feedback matters, practical methods for collecting it, how to analyze and act on it, and the pivotal role transparency plays in building trust and loyalty.

Why Feedback Matters in Offline Marketing

Customer feedback is the cornerstone of any successful business, but its importance is magnified in an offline marketing strategy. Unlike digital platforms where algorithms dictate what you see, offline feedback offers unfiltered, honest insights directly from your customers. This direct connection allows you to understand their needs, preferences, and pain points on a deeper level. Social media metrics might tell you how many people clicked on an ad, but they can't convey the emotional resonance or specific challenges your customers face.

For example, a bakery owner might notice a spike in sales for a particular pastry through digital analytics. However, it's through face-to-face conversations or comment cards that they discover customers love the pastry because it's a healthier option. This insight could lead to a broader marketing campaign focused on health-conscious offerings, something that might have been overlooked in a purely digital strategy.

Feedback also fosters a sense of community. When customers see that their opinions are valued and acted upon, they develop a stronger connection to the brand. This emotional bond is crucial for building a cult-like following, where customers become not just buyers but advocates for your business.

Methods for Collecting Offline Feedback

Collecting feedback offline requires a proactive approach, but the rewards are well worth the effort. One effective method is using in-store comment cards. These can be placed near the checkout counter or in designated feedback areas. To encourage participation, consider offering a small incentive, such as a discount on their next purchase or entry into a monthly draw.

Face-to-face conversations are another powerful tool. Train your staff to engage with customers casually, asking open-ended questions like, "How was your experience today?" or "What could we do better?" These interactions can yield immediate, actionable insights. For instance, a boutique owner might learn from a customer that they'd like to see more sustainable clothing options, prompting a shift in inventory.

Print surveys mailed to customers can also be highly effective, especially for businesses with a loyal customer base. These surveys can be more detailed than in-store cards, allowing for deeper insights. Additionally, hosting feedback sessions at local events or community gatherings can provide a wealth of information while strengthening your ties to the community. Ensure these sessions are welcoming and inclusive, encouraging diverse perspectives.

Analyzing and Acting on Feedback

Once you've collected feedback, the next step is to analyze it and translate it into actionable improvements. Start by organizing the data into categories such as product quality, customer service, and overall experience. Look for recurring themes—these are the areas that need your attention most. For example, if multiple customers mention long wait times, it's a clear indicator that operational efficiency needs to be addressed.

Prioritize changes that align with your business goals and have the potential to make the most significant impact. It's not about addressing every single piece of feedback but focusing on those that will enhance the overall customer experience. A coffee shop owner might receive feedback about the need for more seating. While they can't expand their space immediately, they could rearrange existing furniture to maximize comfort.

Case studies can offer valuable lessons here. Take the example of a local bookstore that received feedback about the lack of diverse genres. By expanding their selection and highlighting these new categories in their marketing, they attracted a broader audience and increased sales. This demonstrates how acting on feedback can lead to tangible business growth.

Building Trust Through Transparency

Transparency is the bridge between collecting feedback and building trust. When customers see that their input leads to real changes, they feel valued and heard. One effective strategy is to publish feedback summaries. Share the most common feedback points and the actions you're taking in response. This could be done through newsletters, in-store posters, or even on your website if you have one.

Showcasing customer-driven changes is another powerful way to build trust. If customer feedback led to a new product line or service, make it known. For instance, a fitness studio could create a campaign around a new class schedule designed based on customer requests, emphasizing their commitment to listening.

Creating opportunities for ongoing dialogue is equally important. Encourage customers to continue providing feedback and make it easy for them to do so. This could be through regular feedback sessions, suggestion boxes, or even casual check-ins during their visits. The goal is to foster a culture of continuous improvement and shared ownership.

Real-world examples illustrate the impact of transparency. A local restaurant that openly shared customer feedback about menu preferences and then introduced new dishes based on that feedback saw a significant increase in customer loyalty. Their patrons felt a sense of ownership and pride in the restaurant's evolution, turning them into brand advocates.

Customer feedback is an invaluable asset for small businesses building a cult brand without relying on social media. It offers authentic insights that digital metrics cannot provide, allowing you to refine your offerings, strengthen customer relationships, and foster loyalty. By collecting feedback through offline channels, analyzing it effectively, and acting on it transparently, you can create a business that truly resonates with your audience.

Remember, the goal isn't just to satisfy customers but to engage them in a meaningful way. When customers feel heard and see their feedback shaping your business, they become more than just buyers—they become partners in your journey. This collaborative approach is the foundation of a cult brand, one that thrives on genuine connections and shared values. Embrace the power of offline feedback, and watch your business grow into something extraordinary.

13

Creating a Cult Brand: The Psychology Behind It

In a world oversaturated with digital noise, the most enduring brands are those that transcend transactions and foster deep, emotional connections with their customers. Cult brands don't just sell products—they inspire devotion, loyalty, and a sense of belonging. For small business owners, this isn't about viral moments or algorithmic tricks. It's about understanding the psychological underpinnings of human connection and applying them in meaningful, offline-first ways.

This chapter explores how to build a cult brand by tapping into the core drivers of loyalty: trust, emotional resonance, and community. We'll examine why these elements matter, how they work, and—most importantly—how you can implement them in your own business without relying on social media.

The Foundations of Brand Loyalty

Brand loyalty isn't just about repeat purchases; it's about creating customers who advocate for you, defend you, and feel a personal stake in your success. At its core, loyalty is built on three psychological principles: trust, consistency, and exclusivity.

Trust is the bedrock. Customers must believe in your reliability, integrity, and commitment to delivering on promises. This is cultivated through consistent actions—whether it's a hand-written thank-you note with every order or a no-questions-asked return policy. Small gestures matter. A local bakery that remembers a customer's favorite pastry or a bookstore that curates personalized recommendations builds trust through attentiveness.

Consistency reinforces trust. Your brand's voice, values, and customer experience should feel cohesive across every touchpoint. If your brand stands for sustainability, for example, that should be evident not just in your products but in your packaging, your partnerships, and even the way you train your staff.

Exclusivity, when used thoughtfully, can deepen loyalty. This doesn't mean elitism—it means creating moments or offerings that make customers feel special. Limited-edition products, invite-only events, or early access to sales can foster a sense of being "in the know." A small coffee roaster might host a monthly cupping session for regulars, turning caffeine into camaraderie.

Building Emotional Connections

People don't buy products; they buy how those products make them feel. Emotional connections transform casual buyers into devoted fans. Storytelling is one of the most powerful tools here. Your brand's story should be authentic, relatable, and infused with purpose. A family-owned hardware store might share its multigenerational history, emphasizing craftsmanship and community support. These narratives resonate because they tap into universal human experiences—heritage, perseverance, belonging.

Personalization is another key. When customers feel seen as individuals, their emotional bond with your brand strengthens. A boutique clothing store that keeps notes on clients' style preferences creates a tailored experience that mass retailers can't match. Even small businesses can leverage this by training staff to remember names, preferences, and past interactions.

Shared values also forge emotional ties. Customers increasingly align with brands that reflect their beliefs. Whether it's environmental responsibility, local sourcing, or fair labor practices, your values should be clear and actionable. A zero-waste grocery store doesn't just sell products—it sells a lifestyle and a set of principles that customers can proudly adopt.

Fostering a Sense of Belonging

The most iconic cult brands don't just have customers—they have communities. Creating a sense of belonging means giving people a shared identity and a space to connect. Inclusivity is critical here. Your brand should be a welcoming hub where diverse individuals feel valued. A running club hosted by a local sneaker shop, for instance, can unite people of all fitness levels under a shared passion.

Rituals and traditions also strengthen community bonds. These can be as simple as a weekly trivia night at a neighborhood pub or an annual customer appreciation day. Rituals create anticipation and tradition, turning one-time buyers into regulars.

Physical spaces matter, even in a digital age. A bookstore with cozy reading nooks or a café with communal tables encourages interaction. These spaces become third places—not home, not work, but somewhere people gather because they feel at ease. For small businesses, fostering these environments can differentiate you from impersonal online competitors.

Practical Applications for Small Businesses

Theory is essential, but action is what creates results. Here's how to apply these principles in your business:

Start with your existing customers. They're your best advocates. Implement a loyalty program that rewards not just spending but engagement—referrals, event attendance, or feedback. A plant nursery might offer a free workshop to customers who bring a friend, incentivizing both loyalty and word-of-mouth marketing.

Host offline events. Whether it's a product launch party, a skill-sharing workshop, or a meet-the-maker session, events create tangible connections. A handmade soap business could host a DIY bath bomb class, turning customers into active participants in the brand's story.

Leverage print media thoughtfully. A well-designed newsletter, postcard, or even a zine can feel more personal than an email. Include behind-the-scenes stories, customer spotlights, or exclusive offers to make recipients feel special.

Finally, empower your team. Employees are your brand ambassadors. Train them to embody your values and build genuine relationships with customers. A barista who remembers a regular's order isn't just efficient—they're reinforcing the emotional fabric of your brand.

Cult brands are built on psychology, not gimmicks. By focusing on trust, emotional connection, and community, small businesses can create lasting loyalty without chasing social media trends. The strategies here aren't about quick wins—they're about fostering relationships that stand the test of time.

Your brand has the potential to become more than a business; it can be a cornerstone of your customers' lives. Start small, stay consistent, and remember: the most powerful marketing is human connection.

14

Networking Without Social Media

In an era where digital interactions dominate, the art of offline networking has become a rare yet invaluable skill. For small business owners, cultivating genuine professional relationships without relying on social media can set you apart in a crowded marketplace. This chapter explores how to build meaningful connections through face-to-face interactions, offering practical strategies to identify opportunities, master in-person communication, and nurture long-term relationships that drive business growth.

The Power of Offline Networking

While digital platforms offer convenience, offline networking provides something far more powerful: trust. Studies from Harvard Business Review show that in-person meetings create deeper emotional connections and foster higher levels of trust compared to virtual interactions. Face-to-face conversations allow for nuanced communication—body language, tone, and spontaneity—that simply can't be replicated through a screen.

For small businesses, offline networking also eliminates the noise of social media algorithms. Instead of competing for attention in a crowded feed, you have the undivided focus of the person in front of you. This is especially valuable in local markets, where community ties and personal recommendations can make or break a business.

Consider the story of Maria, a bakery owner who struggled to gain traction online. By attending local farmers' markets and engaging with customers directly, she built a loyal following that eventually led to partnerships with nearby cafes. Her success wasn't driven by likes or shares but by the authentic relationships she nurtured in person.

Identifying Networking Opportunities

The first step in offline networking is knowing where to look. Not all events are created equal, so focus on those that align with your business goals. Industry conferences, trade shows, and local business meetups are obvious choices, but don't overlook niche gatherings like workshops, charity events, or even hobby-based clubs where potential clients or collaborators might gather.

To assess whether an event is worth your time, ask yourself:
- Who is likely to attend?
- Does this align with my target audience or industry?
- What is the potential for meaningful conversations versus superficial exchanges?

A simple but effective strategy is to prioritize smaller, more intimate gatherings where deeper connections are possible. For example, a boutique owner might find more value in a local artisan fair than a large, generic business expo.

Mastering the Art of Face-to-Face Connection

Walking into a room full of strangers can be intimidating, but with the right approach, you can turn those encounters into valuable relationships. Start with a strong elevator pitch—a concise, compelling introduction that explains who you are, what you do, and why it matters. Keep it under 30 seconds and focus on the problem you solve rather than just your product or service.

Active listening is just as important as speaking. Instead of waiting for your turn to talk, ask open-ended questions and show genuine interest in the other person's work. People remember those who make them feel heard.

Body language also plays a crucial role. Maintain eye contact, offer a firm handshake, and avoid crossing your arms, which can signal disinterest. Small gestures, like nodding or leaning slightly forward, show engagement and encourage a more open dialogue.

If you're nervous about approaching strangers, set a modest goal, such as initiating three meaningful conversations per event. Over time, this practice will build your confidence and expand your network organically.

Nurturing and Expanding Your Network

Networking doesn't end when the event does. The real magic happens in the follow-up. Within 24 to 48 hours, send a personalized email or handwritten note referencing something specific from your conversation. This small effort demonstrates professionalism and keeps you top of mind.

To maintain relationships, schedule periodic check-ins. Share relevant articles, introduce contacts who could benefit from knowing each other, or invite them to industry events. These gestures reinforce your value without being transactional.

Consider creating a simple system to track your connections, such as a spreadsheet with notes on when you last spoke and any follow-up actions. This ensures no relationship falls through the cracks.

Case Studies: Successful Offline Networking in Action

One compelling example is James, a freelance graphic designer who struggled to find clients online. He began attending local creative meetups and struck up conversations with other professionals. Through these interactions, he landed a long-term contract with a marketing firm—all because he took the time to build trust in person.

Another case is Sarah, a financial consultant who volunteered to speak at community workshops. Her expertise and approachability led to referrals and a steady stream of clients who valued her personal touch.

These stories highlight a common theme: offline networking isn't about quick wins but about cultivating relationships that yield sustainable growth.

In a world obsessed with digital metrics, the most meaningful connections often happen offline. By prioritizing face-to-face interactions, small business owners can build trust, foster loyalty, and create opportunities that no algorithm can replicate. Start small, focus on authenticity, and remember that every handshake holds the potential to transform your business. The next time you're tempted to scroll for leads, consider stepping away from the screen—your next big opportunity might be waiting in the real world.

15

Hosting Workshops and Classes

In an era dominated by scrolling, swiping, and fleeting online interactions, hosting workshops and classes offers a refreshing antidote. These in-person events provide a space where your brand can shine through authentic connections, hands-on experiences, and meaningful engagement. For small business owners looking to build a loyal customer base and establish authority in their niche, workshops are a powerful tool. This chapter will guide you through the process of planning, organizing, and executing impactful workshops that align with an offline-first marketing strategy. You'll learn how to create memorable experiences, monetize your events, and avoid common pitfalls—all while fostering a community that fuels your brand's growth.

The Power of In-Person Events for Brand Building

In-person events, particularly workshops and classes, offer unique benefits that digital platforms cannot replicate. They allow you to foster trust, build community, and create authentic connections with your audience. Unlike social media, where algorithms dictate visibility, workshops put you directly in front of your ideal customers. Attendees get to experience your expertise firsthand, leaving with a deeper understanding of your brand values and offerings.

Offline-first marketing leverages these advantages to counteract algorithm fatigue. By focusing on real-world interactions, you reduce reliance on digital platforms and create a more sustainable marketing strategy. Workshops also generate word-of-mouth referrals, as participants are likely to share their experiences with friends and colleagues. This organic buzz can amplify your reach far beyond the event itself.

Planning Your Workshop: From Concept to Execution

The success of any workshop begins with thoughtful planning. Start by defining your objectives. Are you aiming to educate, inspire, or sell? Your goals will shape every aspect of the event, from the content to the format. Next, select a topic that aligns with your brand and resonates with your target audience. For example, a bakery might host a class on decorating seasonal cookies, while a fitness coach could offer a workshop on building a personalized workout routine.

Choosing the right venue is equally important. Consider factors such as location, capacity, and ambiance. A cozy café might be ideal for a creative workshop, while a larger space could better suit a hands-on demonstration. Create a timeline that outlines key milestones, from initial planning to post-event follow-up. Logistical considerations, such as budgeting for materials and marketing the event, should also be addressed early on. Promote your workshop through email newsletters, flyers, and partnerships with local businesses to ensure a strong turnout.

Engaging Participants: Designing Memorable Experiences

An engaging workshop is more than just a lecture; it's an interactive experience that leaves a lasting impression. Craft compelling content that balances information with practical application. For example, if you're teaching a photography workshop, include both tips on composition and opportunities for attendees to practice their skills. Hands-on activities are particularly effective, as they allow participants to apply what they've learned and leave with tangible results.

Fostering a collaborative atmosphere is another key to success. Encourage attendees to share their ideas and ask questions. This not only enhances the learning experience but also creates a sense of community. Be prepared to address participant needs by anticipating common questions and offering personalized guidance. A well-handled Q&A session can solidify your authority and leave attendees feeling valued.

Monetizing Your Workshops: Pricing and Revenue Strategies

Workshops can be a significant revenue stream for your business, but pricing them effectively requires careful consideration. Start by researching competitors and understanding what your target audience is willing to pay. Tiered pricing options, such as offering a basic ticket and a VIP package with additional perks, can cater to different budgets and increase overall revenue. Early bird discounts can incentivize early sign-ups, helping you gauge interest and plan accordingly.

Monetization extends beyond ticket sales. Workshops provide an excellent opportunity to showcase your products or services. For instance, a skincare brand might sell its products during a workshop on skincare routines. Bundling workshop access with a product purchase can further drive sales. Additionally, workshops can serve as lead generation tools. Collect attendee information and follow up with personalized offers or invitations to future events.

Case Studies: Real-World Examples of Workshop Success

To illustrate the potential of workshops, let's explore a few real-world examples. A local pottery studio, "Clay Creations," hosted a series of beginner-friendly classes that quickly sold out. By offering hands-on instruction and a relaxed, welcoming environment, the studio attracted a loyal following. Attendees not only signed up for more classes but also purchased pottery kits and tools, creating a steady revenue stream.

Another example comes from "Green Thumb Gardens," a small business specializing in sustainable gardening. Their workshops on urban gardening techniques drew a diverse audience, from novice gardeners to experienced enthusiasts. By providing actionable tips and fostering a sense of community, the business established itself as a trusted authority in its niche. Attendees frequently returned for additional workshops and recommended them to friends, driving organic growth.

Common Pitfalls and How to Avoid Them

While workshops offer numerous benefits, they come with their own set of challenges. Low attendance can be discouraging, but proactive marketing and strategic partnerships can help mitigate this risk. Ensure your promotional efforts reach the right audience and consider collaborating with complementary businesses to expand your reach.

Logistical issues, such as equipment malfunctions or venue problems, can disrupt your event. A thorough checklist and contingency plan can prevent these mishaps. For example, test all equipment beforehand and have backup supplies on hand. Participant dissatisfaction is another potential pitfall. Solicit feedback during and after the workshop to identify areas for improvement. Addressing concerns promptly and professionally can turn a negative experience into a positive one.

Hosting workshops and classes is a powerful strategy for building a loyal customer base and establishing authority in your niche. By focusing on in-person events, you can create authentic connections, foster community, and generate word-of-mouth referrals—all without relying on social media algorithms. From planning and execution to monetization and follow-up, every aspect of your workshop should reflect your brand values and resonate with your audience.

As you embark on this journey, remember that the success of a workshop lies in its ability to deliver value and create memorable experiences. By applying the strategies outlined in this chapter, you can host events that not only drive revenue but also strengthen your brand's presence in the real world. Embrace the power of offline-first marketing and watch your business flourish through the meaningful, impactful connections forged in your workshops.

16

The Art of Storytelling in Offline Marketing

In a world dominated by digital noise, the power of storytelling remains one of the most effective ways to connect with your audience—without relying on social media. Stories transcend algorithms and fleeting trends. They create emotional bonds, foster trust, and make your brand unforgettable. This chapter will guide you through the art of crafting and delivering compelling narratives that resonate deeply with your customers, whether through events, print media, or community engagement.

The Fundamentals of Storytelling

Every great story begins with authenticity. Your brand's narrative should reflect its core values, mission, and the people behind it. Start by asking yourself: What makes our business unique? What challenges have we overcome? What emotions do we want to evoke in our audience?

A well-structured story follows a clear arc: introduction, conflict, and resolution. For example, a local bakery might share its journey from a family recipe passed down for generations to the opening of its first storefront. The conflict could be the struggle to preserve tradition while adapting to modern tastes, and the resolution is the creation of a menu that honors the past while embracing innovation.

Sensory details bring stories to life. Instead of saying, "Our coffee is rich and flavorful," describe the aroma of freshly roasted beans filling the air, the sound of the grinder humming in the background, and the first warm sip that feels like a morning ritual. These details make your narrative immersive and memorable.

Storytelling in Events

Live events offer a powerful platform for storytelling. Whether you're hosting a product launch, workshop, or pop-up shop, every element should contribute to a cohesive narrative.

Begin with a strong opening that captures attention. A boutique clothing brand might start an event by recounting the inspiration behind its latest collection—perhaps a trip to a vibrant textile market overseas. This sets the tone and gives attendees a deeper connection to the products.

Speaker selection is crucial. Choose individuals who embody your brand's story, whether it's the founder, a longtime employee, or a loyal customer. Their genuine passion will resonate more than a scripted sales pitch.

Interactive elements deepen engagement. For instance, a bookstore could host a "storytelling hour" where customers share their favorite literary memories, weaving their experiences into the brand's narrative. These moments create shared memories and strengthen community ties.

Connecting Through Print Media

Print media offers a tangible, lasting way to tell your story. Brochures, newsletters, and direct mail pieces should be more than just promotional—they should invite readers into your brand's world.

A well-designed newsletter might feature a "Behind the Scenes" section, revealing the craftsmanship that goes into your products. A local farm could share seasonal updates, complete with photos of the harvest and stories about the farmers who grow the food. This approach transforms mundane updates into compelling narratives.

Direct mail can be particularly effective when it feels personal. A handwritten note accompanying a sample product, explaining why it was chosen for the recipient, adds a layer of thoughtfulness that digital communication often lacks.

Case studies of successful print storytelling can inspire your strategy. Consider how Patagonia's catalogs double as storytelling vehicles, featuring essays on environmental activism alongside product showcases. This alignment of values and narrative strengthens brand loyalty.

Building Community Through Storytelling

Stories have the power to unite people around shared values and experiences. Your brand can become a hub for community by highlighting collective narratives.

Hosting local storytelling nights is one way to foster connection. A hardware store might invite customers to share DIY project stories, celebrating creativity and problem-solving. These events position your business as a gathering place, not just a retailer.

Collaborations with other small businesses can amplify your impact. A café and a bookstore might team up for a "Literary Brunch" series, where authors discuss their work over coffee and pastries. These partnerships create richer stories than any business could tell alone.

Highlight customer stories in your marketing. Feature testimonials that go beyond generic praise, instead sharing how your product or service played a meaningful role in someone's life. A fitness studio could showcase a member's journey to wellness, emphasizing the community support that made it possible.

Advanced Storytelling Techniques

Once you've mastered the basics, elevate your storytelling with these advanced strategies.

Serialized narratives keep audiences coming back for more. A quarterly magazine or newsletter can unfold a story over time, like a behind-the-scenes look at developing a new product line. This builds anticipation and sustained engagement.

Multimedia elements enhance print and event storytelling. Include QR codes in brochures that link to audio clips of team members sharing their favorite brand memories. At events, use projection screens to display customer photos and stories in real time.

Measure the impact of your efforts. Track event attendance, newsletter open rates, and customer feedback to see which stories resonate most. Adjust your approach based on what works, but always stay true to your brand's authentic voice.

Storytelling is not just a marketing tool—it's the heartbeat of your brand. By crafting authentic, emotionally resonant narratives, you can forge deeper connections with your audience, whether through events, print media, or community building. The best stories linger in the mind long after the last page is turned or the event ends. In a world where attention is scarce, storytelling ensures your brand is not just seen, but remembered. Start small, stay consistent, and watch as your stories transform customers into lifelong advocates.

17

Integrating Offline Marketing into Your Plan

In an era dominated by digital noise, offline marketing remains a powerful tool for small businesses aiming to build a cult brand. While social media can feel like an endless scroll of fleeting attention, offline strategies offer tangible, memorable experiences that foster deeper connections with your audience. This chapter will guide you through the process of integrating offline marketing into your business plan, ensuring your efforts are aligned with your goals, budget-friendly, and measurable.

Aligning Offline Marketing with Business Goals

The first step in any successful marketing strategy is alignment. Offline efforts should never exist in isolation; they must support your broader business objectives. Begin by identifying your key goals—whether it's increasing brand awareness, driving foot traffic, or building customer loyalty. Once these are clear, map your offline initiatives to these goals.

For example, if your objective is to strengthen community ties, consider hosting a local event or sponsoring a neighborhood project. If brand awareness is your priority, a well-placed print ad in a niche magazine or a strategically designed billboard could be more effective than a generic social media post. The goal is to ensure every offline campaign reinforces your long-term vision.

Start by asking:
- What specific outcomes do I want from my marketing efforts?
- How can offline tactics uniquely achieve these outcomes?
- What resources (time, money, personnel) am I willing to commit?

By answering these questions, you'll create a cohesive marketing plan where offline and online efforts complement rather than compete with each other.

Budgeting for Offline Marketing

One of the biggest misconceptions about offline marketing is that it's prohibitively expensive. While some tactics, like TV commercials or full-page magazine spreads, can strain a small business's budget, there are countless cost-effective alternatives. The key is to prioritize creativity and strategic thinking over sheer spending power.

Consider grassroots campaigns, such as handing out branded merchandise at local events or partnering with complementary businesses for joint promotions. Print media, often dismissed as outdated, can be highly effective when used thoughtfully—think postcards mailed to a targeted neighborhood or eye-catching flyers placed in high-traffic areas.

To stay on track, create a detailed budget that accounts for all potential expenses, from printing costs to event permits. Use the following framework:

1. Fixed Costs: Expenses that don't change, like venue rentals or ad placements.
2. Variable Costs: Items that scale with your campaign, such as printing more flyers or increasing giveaway quantities.

3. Hidden Costs: Often overlooked, like staff time or transportation.

A well-planned budget ensures you maximize impact without overspending, allowing you to test and refine your approach over time.

Measuring and Evaluating ROI

Without measurable results, even the most creative offline campaigns can feel like shots in the dark. Tracking ROI is essential to understanding what works and justifying future investments. Start by defining clear KPIs tailored to your goals.

For brand awareness, track metrics like event attendance, press mentions, or coupon redemptions. For sales-driven campaigns, monitor direct revenue linked to promo codes or in-store mentions of your offline ads. Simple tools like customer surveys or QR codes on print materials can bridge the gap between offline efforts and measurable data.

Once you've collected data, analyze it to identify trends. Did a particular event drive more repeat customers? Did a print ad in a local paper outperform a radio spot? Use these insights to refine your strategy, doubling down on what works and pivoting away from what doesn't.

Case Studies: Lessons from Successful Brands

Real-world examples illustrate the power of offline marketing. Take the case of a small bakery that built a cult following by hosting monthly "secret menu" tastings for loyal customers. By creating an exclusive, in-person experience, they fostered a sense of community that no Instagram post could replicate.

Another example is a boutique clothing store that partnered with local artists to host pop-up shops in unconventional venues, like abandoned warehouses or parks. These events generated buzz, press coverage, and a devoted customer base—all without a single paid social media ad.

These cases highlight a common thread: offline marketing thrives on authenticity and creativity. When you give people something memorable to experience, they become not just customers, but advocates.

Avoiding Common Pitfalls

Even the best-laid plans can stumble if you overlook common pitfalls. One major mistake is underestimating costs—what starts as a "simple" event can quickly balloon with unforeseen expenses. Always build a buffer into your budget.

Another misstep is failing to measure results. Without tracking, you'll never know which efforts are worth repeating. Implement systems to capture data from day one.

Finally, avoid inauthentic community engagement. Customers can spot insincerity a mile away. If you're sponsoring a local event or partnering with another business, ensure your involvement aligns with your brand values and resonates with your audience.

Offline marketing isn't a relic of the past—it's a timeless strategy for building a cult brand in a digital world. By aligning your efforts with business goals, budgeting wisely, measuring ROI, and learning from successful brands, you can create campaigns that leave a lasting impression. Remember, the most powerful marketing doesn't just capture attention; it builds relationships. And in an age of endless scrolling, those relationships are your greatest competitive advantage.

Now it's your turn. Start small, stay consistent, and watch as your offline efforts transform your business into something truly unscrollable.

18

Building a Loyal Customer Base Offline

In an era dominated by digital noise, cultivating a loyal customer base without relying on social media may seem daunting. Yet, some of the most enduring brands have thrived by focusing on offline strategies that foster genuine connections. This chapter explores how small business owners can build sustainable loyalty through personalized experiences, effective loyalty programs, and retention strategies that prioritize face-to-face interactions. By embracing these offline tactics, you can create a community of devoted customers who not only return but also become advocates for your brand.

The Power of Personalized Experiences

Personalization is the cornerstone of customer loyalty. When customers feel seen and valued, they are more likely to return and recommend your business to others. Simple gestures, like remembering a customer's name or their favorite product, can leave a lasting impression. These small acts of thoughtfulness signal that your business cares about their individual needs and preferences.

One effective way to personalize customer interactions is through handwritten thank-you notes. While it may seem old-fashioned, the tactile nature of a handwritten note makes it stand out in a world dominated by digital communication. For example, a boutique owner could include a personalized note with every purchase, thanking the customer and offering a tailored recommendation for their next visit.

Another powerful tactic is offering exclusive in-store experiences. Consider hosting events where loyal customers can preview new products or enjoy private shopping hours. These experiences not only reward repeat customers but also reinforce their connection to your brand.

Research consistently highlights the emotional impact of personalized service. Studies show that customers are more likely to develop an emotional attachment to a brand when they feel their individuality is acknowledged. By focusing on these small, meaningful interactions, you can create a sense of belonging that keeps customers coming back.

Designing Effective Customer Loyalty Programs

Customer loyalty programs are a proven way to incentivize repeat business, but they don't have to rely on digital platforms. Offline loyalty programs can be just as effective—if not more so—in fostering customer retention. The key is to design programs that are simple, rewarding, and aligned with your brand values.

Tiered rewards systems are a popular option. For instance, customers could earn points for every purchase, with rewards escalating as they reach higher tiers. A local coffee shop might offer a free drink after ten purchases, followed by a complimentary pastry after twenty. This approach encourages repeat visits while offering tangible benefits that customers appreciate.

Membership cards are another effective tool. Physical cards can be stamped with each purchase, providing a visible reminder of progress toward a reward. This tangible element adds a sense of achievement that digital systems often lack. Additionally, referral systems can amplify word-of-mouth marketing. Encourage loyal customers to refer friends by offering discounts or exclusive perks for both parties.

Case studies reveal the success of offline loyalty programs. For example, a neighborhood bookstore implemented a punch card system that rewarded customers with a free book after ten purchases. This simple yet effective program not only boosted repeat sales but also strengthened the bookstore's ties to its community. By designing loyalty programs that align with your brand and customer preferences, you can create a powerful incentive for repeat business.

Retention Strategies That Build Community

Building a loyal customer base goes beyond transactions—it's about fostering a sense of community. Customers are more likely to return when they feel connected to your brand and to each other. Hosting events is an excellent way to achieve this. Workshops, networking nights, and exclusive previews provide opportunities for customers to engage with your brand in meaningful ways.

Consider organizing events that align with your products or services. A cooking supply store could host monthly cooking classes, while a fitness studio might offer free community workout sessions. These events not only showcase your expertise but also create memorable experiences that strengthen customer loyalty.

Consistent, high-quality service is another critical factor in retention. Train your team to deliver exceptional customer experiences, whether it's through attentive service, knowledgeable recommendations, or timely follow-ups. Customers are more likely to return when they know they can rely on your business for outstanding service.

Listening to customer feedback is equally important. Use surveys or informal conversations to gather insights about their preferences and experiences. Actively incorporating their feedback demonstrates that you value their input and are committed to meeting their needs. For example, a local bakery adjusted its offerings based on customer requests for gluten-free options, resulting in increased loyalty among health-conscious patrons.

Leveraging Print Media and Local Outreach

Print media remains a powerful tool for staying connected with customers offline. Flyers, newsletters, and postcards offer tangible reminders of your brand that digital communications often lack. Well-designed print materials can capture attention and provide valuable information in a format that customers can hold onto.

When designing print media, focus on simplicity and clarity. Highlight upcoming events, new products, or special promotions in a visually appealing way. For example, a boutique could send out seasonal postcards featuring new arrivals and an invitation to an exclusive sale event. This approach not only keeps customers informed but also creates anticipation and excitement.

Local outreach is another effective strategy. Partnering with community organizations or sponsoring local events can increase your visibility and credibility. For instance, a hardware store might sponsor a community garden project, reinforcing its commitment to the neighborhood while attracting like-minded customers. These partnerships demonstrate that your business is invested in the community, fostering goodwill and loyalty.

Measuring Offline Customer Loyalty Success

Tracking the effectiveness of your offline loyalty strategies is essential for refining your approach and maximizing results. While offline metrics may require more effort to collect than digital analytics, they provide valuable insights into customer behavior and satisfaction.

One key metric is repeat purchase rates. Track how often customers return to make additional purchases, as this indicates the strength of their loyalty. Customer feedback is another crucial source of information. Use surveys, focus groups, or informal conversations to gather insights about their experiences and preferences.

Manual tracking systems, such as punch cards or membership records, can also provide valuable data. These tools allow you to monitor customer activity and identify trends that inform your strategy. For example, if a particular reward program drives significant repeat business, consider expanding it to offer additional incentives.

Interpreting this data requires a balance of intuition and analysis. Look for patterns that indicate what's working and where improvements are needed. If customers consistently mention the importance of personalized service, invest in training your team to enhance these interactions. By regularly reviewing and adjusting your strategies, you can ensure that your efforts continue to resonate with your audience.

Building a loyal customer base offline is not only possible but also deeply rewarding. By focusing on personalized experiences, effective loyalty programs, and community-building strategies, you can create lasting connections that transcend the digital realm. Print media and local outreach further amplify your efforts, keeping your brand visible and relevant within your community.

As you implement these strategies, remember that loyalty is built through consistency and authenticity. Customers value businesses that prioritize their needs and demonstrate genuine care. By committing to these offline tactics, you can cultivate a loyal customer base that sustains your business for years to come. In a world increasingly dominated by digital interactions, the power of face-to-face connections remains unmatched—and it's within your reach to harness it.

19

The Future of Offline Marketing

In an era where digital noise is overwhelming and algorithms dictate visibility, small business owners are rediscovering the power of offline marketing. While social media and digital ads once promised endless reach, they now often deliver diminishing returns, leaving entrepreneurs searching for more authentic ways to connect with their audiences. This chapter explores the resurgence of offline marketing as a strategic response to algorithm fatigue, offering actionable insights into emerging trends, shifting consumer behaviors, and innovative ways to stay competitive in a digitally saturated world.

The Resurgence of Offline Marketing

The digital revolution promised efficiency and scale, but it also created an unexpected side effect: a longing for real-world connection. Consumers today are exhausted by endless scrolling, targeted ads, and the impersonal nature of online interactions. This fatigue has led to a renewed appreciation for tangible, offline experiences that engage the senses and foster genuine human connections.

Offline marketing isn't just nostalgic—it's psychologically powerful. Studies show that physical interactions, such as touching a product or engaging in face-to-face conversations, activate emotional responses that digital experiences can't replicate. For example, receiving a beautifully designed direct mail piece feels more personal than an email, and attending a live event creates memories that a social media post can't match. These experiences build deeper brand loyalty because they engage customers on a multisensory level, making your business more memorable.

The limitations of digital platforms are also driving this shift. Algorithm changes can wipe out a brand's visibility overnight, and ad costs continue to rise. In contrast, offline strategies—whether through print media, community partnerships, or in-person events—offer stability and control. By investing in offline marketing, small businesses can reduce their reliance on unpredictable digital platforms and create lasting impressions that stand the test of time.

Emerging Trends in Offline Strategies

As offline marketing regains momentum, innovative trends are reshaping how businesses engage with their audiences. One standout strategy is the rise of experiential events. Pop-up shops, workshops, and immersive brand activations allow customers to interact with your products or services in a meaningful way. For example, a local coffee roaster might host a tasting event where attendees learn about brewing techniques while sampling new blends. These experiences not only drive sales but also create advocates who share their experiences organically—both online and offline.

Direct mail is another trend making a comeback. In a world flooded with digital ads, a well-crafted postcard or handwritten note stands out. The key is personalization. A boutique clothing store, for instance, could send exclusive preview invites to loyal customers, making them feel valued and increasing the likelihood of a visit. Combining direct mail with QR codes or personalized URLs can also bridge the gap between offline and online, allowing you to track engagement and refine future campaigns.

Community engagement is also proving to be a powerful offline strategy. Sponsoring local events, partnering with neighboring businesses, or hosting charity drives not only boosts visibility but also strengthens your brand's reputation. Consumers increasingly prefer businesses that contribute to their communities, and these efforts often generate word-of-mouth referrals—a form of marketing that's both free and highly trusted.

Adapting to Changing Consumer Behaviors

Understanding how consumer behaviors are evolving is critical to crafting effective offline strategies. Today's customers crave authenticity and meaningful interactions, which is why they're gravitating toward brands that prioritize real-world engagement. For small businesses, this means paying attention to where and how your audience spends their time offline.

Start by identifying your customers' offline habits. Do they frequent farmers' markets, attend local networking events, or subscribe to niche print magazines? Aligning your marketing efforts with these behaviors ensures your message reaches them in a context they already value. For example, a wellness coach might distribute flyers at yoga studios or offer free workshops at community centers, meeting potential clients where they're already engaged.

Another shift is the growing preference for slow, intentional consumption. In contrast to the instant gratification of online shopping, many consumers now appreciate the deliberateness of offline purchases. A bookstore that hosts author readings or a bakery that offers in-person baking classes taps into this desire for deeper engagement. By creating opportunities for customers to slow down and connect, you position your brand as an antidote to the fast-paced digital world.

Staying Ahead of the Curve

The most successful businesses don't choose between offline and online—they integrate both seamlessly. The future of marketing lies in blending the tactile appeal of offline strategies with the data-driven precision of digital tools. For instance, an offline event can be promoted through social media, while attendee data collected at the event can inform future email campaigns. This hybrid approach maximizes reach and impact.

Measuring the ROI of offline efforts is essential. While digital campaigns offer instant metrics, offline strategies require a different approach. Use unique promo codes, custom landing pages, or post-event surveys to track engagement. For example, a restaurant hosting a pop-up dinner might offer a discount code for future visits, allowing you to measure how many attendees converted into repeat customers.

Innovation also means staying open to experimentation. Test different offline tactics—whether it's guerrilla marketing, local partnerships, or print ads—and analyze what resonates with your audience. The businesses that thrive will be those willing to adapt, iterate, and find creative ways to stand out in an increasingly noisy world.

Offline marketing is no longer a relic of the past—it's a vital strategy for the future. As digital fatigue grows, small businesses that invest in real-world connections will differentiate themselves and build lasting customer loyalty. By embracing experiential events, leveraging emerging trends like direct mail, and aligning with shifting consumer behaviors, you can create meaningful brand experiences that transcend the limitations of digital platforms.

The key is balance. While digital tools offer efficiency, offline strategies provide depth and authenticity. By integrating both, you future-proof your marketing efforts and ensure your brand remains relevant in an ever-changing landscape. The businesses that succeed won't just compete in the marketplace—they'll create communities, foster relationships, and leave a lasting impression that no algorithm can erase.

20

Conclusion: Embracing the Unscrollable Movement

As we reach the final chapter of Unscrollable: How to Build a Cult Brand Without Social Media, it's time to reflect on the journey we've taken together. The Unscrollable Movement is more than just a marketing strategy; it's a mindset shift that prioritizes genuine human connections over fleeting online interactions. In a world where algorithms dictate visibility and engagement, building a cult brand offline is not only possible—it's profoundly rewarding. This chapter serves as a recap of the key principles we've explored and a roadmap to help you take actionable steps toward embracing the Unscrollable ethos.

Recap: The Pillars of Unscrollable Branding

Throughout this book, we've delved into the foundational strategies of offline-first marketing. These pillars are designed to help you create a brand that resonates deeply with your audience, fostering loyalty and authenticity. Let's revisit them briefly:

1. Organizing Local Events: Hosting workshops, pop-up shops, or community gatherings allows you to connect with your audience face-to-face. These events create memorable experiences that social media simply can't replicate. Start small by identifying spaces in your commu-

nity where you can host an event, and focus on creating an atmosphere that reflects your brand's values.

2. Utilizing Print Media: From business cards to flyers, print materials offer a tangible way to leave a lasting impression. Design pieces that are visually striking and convey your brand's story. Consider local newspapers or magazines as platforms for reaching your audience in a meaningful way.

3. Fostering Community Partnerships: Collaborating with other local businesses or organizations can amplify your reach and strengthen your brand's presence. Look for partners who share your values and can help you create mutually beneficial initiatives.

4. Creating Memorable Offline Experiences: Whether it's through thoughtful packaging, handwritten notes, or personalized service, small touches can make a big difference. These experiences build emotional connections that turn customers into advocates.

Each of these strategies reinforces the idea that marketing doesn't have to be digital to be impactful. By investing in offline-first approaches, you're building a brand that stands the test of time.

Taking Action: Your Unscrollable Roadmap

Now that you're familiar with the pillars of Unscrollable branding, it's time to put them into practice. Here's a step-by-step roadmap to help you get started:

1. Identify Community Touchpoints: Start by mapping out the places and spaces where your target audience spends time. This could be local coffee shops, community centers, or even parks. Understanding these touchpoints will help you plan where to focus your efforts.

2. Plan Your First Local Event: Choose a venue, set a date, and outline the purpose of your event. Whether it's a product launch or a workshop, ensure the event aligns with your brand's identity. Don't forget to promote it through word-of-mouth and print materials.

3. Design Your Print Materials: Work with a designer or use online tools to create high-quality print materials. Keep your brand's aesthetic consistent and include a clear call to action. Distribute these materials strategically at your event or in community spaces.

4. Build Partnerships: Reach out to local businesses or organizations that align with your brand. Propose collaborative projects, such as co-hosted events or joint marketing campaigns. These partnerships can help you tap into new audiences.

5. Focus on Experiences: Think about how you can surprise and delight your customers in person. Small gestures, like a handwritten thank-you note or a complimentary sample, can leave a lasting impression.

Remember, starting small is key. Pick one strategy to focus on initially, and gradually expand as you gain confidence and momentum.

Overcoming Challenges and Staying Committed

Embracing the Unscrollable Movement may come with its share of challenges. Initial costs, skepticism about offline marketing, or the fear of stepping away from the digital realm are common concerns. But these challenges are not insurmountable.

For instance, while print materials require an upfront investment, they often yield a higher return in terms of brand loyalty and customer engagement. If budget is a concern, start with simple designs or collaborate with local printers who may offer discounts for small businesses.

Skepticism from peers or customers is another hurdle. Combat this by sharing success stories from brands that have thrived offline, and be transparent about your journey. Over time, the authenticity of your approach will speak for itself.

Staying committed to offline-first marketing requires patience and perseverance. It's not about immediate results but about building a foundation that will sustain your brand for years to come. Celebrate small wins along the way, and remind yourself of the long-term benefits of cultivating real-world connections.

The Unscrollable Mindset: Beyond Marketing

The Unscrollable Movement is more than just a marketing strategy—it's a way of life. By prioritizing analog connections, you're not only transforming your business but also enriching your personal life. In a world dominated by screens and notifications, embracing offline interactions fosters a sense of presence and authenticity.

This mindset extends beyond branding. It's about slowing down, being intentional, and valuing the people and experiences that truly matter. When you apply this philosophy to your business, you create a ripple effect that touches your community and beyond.

As you move forward, remember that the Unscrollable ethos is about redefining success. It's not about likes, shares, or followers but about the impact you make in the real world. By choosing to build your cult brand offline, you're taking a stand against the noise of the digital age and embracing a more meaningful approach to marketing.

Final Thoughts

The Unscrollable Movement is a call to return to the roots of connection—to the moments that remind us of our humanity. In a society increasingly dominated by technology, building a cult brand without social media is a radical act of authenticity. It's a testament to the enduring power of face-to-face interactions, tangible experiences, and genuine relationships.

As you embark on this journey, remember that you're not alone. Countless businesses have found success by embracing offline-first strategies, and you can too. Start small, stay committed, and trust in the process. The Unscrollable Movement isn't just about building a brand—it's about creating a legacy rooted in authenticity and connection.

Thank you for joining us on this journey. Now, it's your turn to take the first step toward embracing the Unscrollable ethos. Your brand, your community, and your life will be better for it.